Love, Light, Laughter

The New Spirituality

Owen Waters

About This Book

Love, Light, Laughter: The New Spirituality goes far beyond basic spiritual awakening. It reveals exactly what developments to expect after you have stepped into the spiritual stages of consciousness.

While heart-centered consciousness is the doorway to spirituality, it is becoming apparent to millions of people today that there is much more to be found and experienced beyond this first stage. Once people allow the unconditional love that will naturally fill their hearts, they go on to find the light that streams continually outwards from their very souls – filling their beings with inspiration.

Within the light, they discover the laughter – the joy of spiritual contact which offers happiness regardless of any external circumstances.

The hallmarks of the New Spirituality are love, light, and laughter. They are the stages of spiritual consciousness which will form the basis of the building of a New Reality. They are the seeds of a greater awareness, a greater love, and a greater understanding for all of the people upon the Earth.

The world is changing. Discover exactly where the Great Change will lead by reading this vital and timely book.

About the Author

Owen Waters is an international spiritual teacher who has helped hundreds of thousands of spiritual seekers to understand better the nature of their inner being and their infinite potential. In 1963, at the age of 13, his interest in metaphysics started when he experienced a profound, out-of-body spiritual awakening. Since then, his life has been focused on gaining spiritual insights through extensive research and the development of his inner connection to higher states of consciousness.

Waters' first book, *The Shift: The Revolution in Human Consciousness,* was published in November 2005 in hardcover, and it went on to sell more than 5,000 copies, largely through word-of-mouth recommendation. He then wrote the e-book, *Discover Your Purpose in Life,* after being given the answer to the oldest mystery on earth – *why* the universe was created.

He went on to write the e-book, *Freedom of the Spirit: Four Powerful Steps to Spiritual Freedom,* which combines four of today's most proven and time-tested spiritual practices into one powerful and effective package.

As a service to the spiritual community, Waters offered his next e-book free of charge on his InfiniteBeing.com web site.

The title of this book, *Love, Light, Laughter*, focuses on today's emerging stages of consciousness. These stages encompass unconditional love, the light of knowledge obtained through inspiration, and the joy of contact with the powerful creativity of your soul.

Table of Contents

*In the New Reality,
success will be measured,
not by money, but by the
amount of joy in your life.*

~ Owen Waters

Introduction

Love, light, and laughter refer to the three stages of consciousness which are unfolding in today's emerging age of New Spirituality. These stages of consciousness are:

- Heart-centered awareness
- Inspiration from your soul consciousness
- The joy that comes through contact with your soul

Heart-centered awareness opens up a whole new world of mutual trust and support. It creates well-being from the inside out and draws people to your side who quickly become your close friends. Heart-centered awareness is the doorway through which you enter the spiritual realms of awareness. It is the doorway to your own spiritual experiences and your own personal inspiration.

Contact with your inner being or soul consciousness provides constant inspiration in handling every type of situation. At the core of your inner being, you are attuned to the true energy of every person and every situation. This gives you the ability to know intuitively which decisions will work out the best. You find yourself saying that familiar phrase, "I just know," more and more often. One of the greatest secrets to success in human living is to allow inspiration from within to enter into your daily awareness.

Love, Light, Laughter

Your connection with your soul consciousness or inner being also connects you with the pure sense of joy which constantly flows from the Creator throughout all of life. The universe, by design, is filled with an uplifting, unconditional love which radiates from the Divine source and cascades throughout every realm of manifestation. It is your birthright to experience inner joy, and it is never further than a thought away.

Once people discover the unconditional love which constantly flows into their hearts, they explore further and find the light of inspiration that streams from their very soul. Within that light, they discover the "laughter" – the sense of joy which comes from spiritual contact; the sense of joy which fills their very being regardless of all external circumstances.

This book will help you see the way ahead and help you to acquire the ability to fill your life with love, light, and the laughter of the spiritual joy that flows from within your being.

The Secret of Personal Magnetism

The Secret of Personal Magnetism

When people open their hearts to unselfish, uncondi-tional love, a whole new world of possibilities opens. Rather than spending effort avoiding the selfishness of others, they spend time making sure that the way they choose to serve society is done in the best way possible. When people can trust others to treat each other with love and respect rather than as competitors, then every-one gains.

As heart-centered awareness grows and blooms within society, people's primary focus will shift away from ser-vice to self and towards service to others. When it does, the world will transform out of all recognition.

But you don't have to wait for all of society to catch up. In both your personal and professional dealings with people, you have a reputation, and it is fed by word-of-mouth recommendation. Build your reputation as someone who tends to give more than is expected of them, and you will find yourself becoming increasingly popular in both your business and personal lives. People respond to heartfelt action and, as they say, what goes around comes around.

Love, Light, Laughter

Action and reaction are opposite and equal in all types of thought and action. Your heartfelt action, by automatic reaction, will create a heartfelt reality among you and the people who are attracted to your energy. When you operate mainly out of a heart-centered frequency, you will notice that people are attracted to you in all aspects of your life. Friends, lovers, professional associates; everyone will be attracted to your magnetic personality.

Personal magnetism has been one of the great mysteries of life simply because, in the past, so few people have operated from that heart-centered frequency of awareness on a routine basis. However, it's really no secret. It's just one of those common-sense facts of life.

The secret of personal magnetism is that the more you unconditionally love people, the more they love you.

You don't have to make a big deal out of it. You don't have to stand there like some transmitter beacon, radiating huge amounts of heart energy. Top stage performers do, but you don't. You can be very quiet about it and everyone will be quietly drawn to you. Everyone of a similar nature, that is. Everyone who appreciates kindness and a truly warm, genuine smile.

In other words, you'll attract the very best of friends.

There's nothing more attractive than a warm smile from a person who quietly radiates a sense of unconditional love for themselves and all others.

Accessing Inner Wisdom

Accessing Inner Wisdom

Inspiration comes from contact with your soul consciousness. It's always available simply for the asking and, through the practice of daily meditation, you expand your ability to receive impressions from your inner being. Bear in mind that your inner being has access to a much wider perspective of any situation than your conscious mind can grasp. Your conscious mind's focus is on the outside world and the five major physical senses, while your inner being has access to the very core of a situation.

Your inner being perceives the total energy of every situation and it can project many possible solutions through time to see how each one would turn out. You can learn to access this higher intelligence and insight with even just a few minutes a day spent practicing inner communion through meditation. When you do this, you can then see the most practical and elegant solution to any circumstances.

With inspiration from your inner being, you become a person who appears to have greater wisdom. Whether you are being given greater wisdom or simply greater knowledge about a particular situation doesn't really matter. The effect is still the same – *you tend to get things right the first time.*

Love, Light, Laughter

Great wisdom does exist within each and every one of us, and you only have to ask for it to discover that it was there all the time. The inner wisdom was just waiting for your conscious mind to discover it as a resource.

Many years ago, I attended a self-discovery workshop, and we all paired off to work with a partner in an experiment to discover our inner wisdom. We were supposed to turn to our partner, a total stranger, and *act as though* we were a very wise being. Your partner would ask you for advice on an issue that they faced in their life and ask for your wisdom and insight as to how to best handle it.

Now I must confess that I'm the world's worst actor because I have a huge blockage in that direction. If I try to portray anything that isn't me, I can't get past an aversion to pretending to be something that I'm not. I know this from past experience. I did an acting class once – for an entire hour – and I couldn't wait to get out of there.

That day in the self-discovery workshop, however, I did eventually discover a way past this blockage accidentally. But initially, there I was, blocked and feeling distracted and embarrassed, while I was supposed to be acting like some kind of wise oracle.

As my partner asked me for advice and wisdom, I could tell that the issue was real and bothered him deeply. He really was seeking some kind of insight into how to handle it. So, for his sake, I resolved to do my best and my desire to help started to melt my self-conscious blockage.

I started coming up with useful information that might

help him. But then I ran out of immediate ideas and I just didn't know where to turn next. If this was some test of my ability to act out the scene, I could just imagine a movie set director lurking in the background, getting ready to yell, "Cut!" and send me off the set.

Desperate for inspiration, I fell back into my inner being, and that is where that I found the answers. From within myself came the sweetest words of support and healing wisdom that I had heard in a long, long time. Once I gave up the conscious struggle and the emotional hang-up that was blocking the way, out came the real light that shines within each and every one of us.

Wow, was I impressed! So was my partner. He started looking at me as if somebody as wise as Jesus was speaking through my mouth! That made me feel embarrassed again, which stopped the whole process; however, the objective had already been achieved. My partner had the insight that he sought and I joined the ranks of those who have discovered, for themselves, the wisdom that lies within us all.

In order to tap into your inner wisdom, you don't have to *act as if* or do anything that feels fake in any way. Just know that such wisdom is an attribute of your inner being. It's already there for the asking; so when you need the best kind of guidance, *ask for it* from deep within you. Then watch your conscious mind light up with ideas as they flow into your awareness. You'll be too busy thinking, "Yes, of course!" to all the insights that start emerging to stop and marvel at the incredible depth of wisdom that comes from your eternal soul.

Love, Light, Laughter

As a part of the experience humanity has chosen on Earth, we have been operating in a state of spiritual amnesia. We have a spiritual connection within, but we find ourselves focusing on the outside world to the exclusion of that inner awareness. The point of the exercise in being human is to rediscover how to tune into your own soul or higher consciousness and benefit from the vast resources of its wisdom of the ages.

You are here to raise your consciousness above the old limitations, to reconnect with your spiritual nature, and to discover the love, light, and spiritual joy that spring from your inner being. The more you do this, the more you will join the growing refrain of spiritual seekers everywhere who say:

"Isn't life *wonderful?*"

The Joy of a Soul Connection

The Joy of a Soul Connection

When we tune into the soul level of consciousness, we discover that there is much more to achieving personal happiness than to anything related to external events. Real joy comes from within, from an unending source which is divine in origin.

The creative will of the Divine Father aspect of God merged in perfect union with the everlasting love of the Divine Mother aspect of God together fill the universe with total, unadulterated, blissful joy!

The greatest discovery of a person who regularly practices meditation is that, one day, the door will open to this unending supply of blissful joy. On that day, the spiritual seeker knows, beyond all shadow of any doubt, that God lies silently within all things and all consciousness. We are a part of that Divine Oneness, and it is through the joy of soul consciousness that we realize this connection.

Remember that your soul consciousness is your complete, inner consciousness. Your daily, conscious awareness, on the other hand, is focused on the outside world for a purpose. The true purpose is so that we can find our way back to that from which we came, even though

25

we are spiritually "blindfolded," so to speak. The game of life on Earth is played so that we can experience the rediscovery of that joyous connection to the oneness from which we originally came.

All the happiness in the world pales in comparison with the supreme joy of that inner connection. Soul-inspired joy is lasting happiness. It has no beginning and no end because it is always there, just as God is always there, within each and every one of us.

Principles of Powerful Creativity

Principles of Powerful Creativity

When you tune into soul consciousness, you become better able to engage in true, powerful creativity. Basic creativity is the application of known elements to produce something in a new way. True, soul-based creativity gathers the forces of the universe together and orchestrates entire new realities. It creates situations that flow into being, molding physical circumstances from pure intention.

Your conscious mind has its purpose and its list of functions. Likewise, your soul consciousness has its purpose and its list of functions. When people learn about creating a new reality through the power of intention or the principle of attraction, they often assume that the conscious mind does the creating. It doesn't. Powerful creativity is a function of the soul level of consciousness. Your inner being does the creating in concert with the intentions of your conscious mind.

First, your conscious mind sets the intention. Then your inner being performs the creative function. Finally, your conscious mind takes action on each impression that comes from within. These impressions provide guidance as you take each step in the process of enabling your vision to come forth into physical reality.

The Law of Creation, in its simplest essence, is:

Creation = Thought + Feeling + Motion

Creation myths from around the world often mention a dividing of the "waters" of original consciousness. This means that consciousness was separated into two complementary types – *thought and feeling* – so that they could be placed into motion in a way that they interact with each other.

How To Create a Better Life

The Law of Creation was powerful enough to build an entire universe, so it can be used by anyone just as effectively to create any new reality that they desire.

Here are the three essential components:

1. Thought, or intent, is used to define the goal, or the desired outcome. To create a better reality in your life, you first consciously specify what you want using intellectual thought.

When defining a goal, it is better to define encompassing generalities rather than limiting the idea by using too many specific details. This allows the universe to find the easiest pathway through which to manifest the desired goal. General principles are better than specific objects. For example, the general principle of natural abundance can find thousands of avenues through which to materialize, whereas a goal involving one specific objective along the path to abundance, such as a shiny new car, narrows the options considerably.

2. Feeling is added to give the goal the life energy with which to grow from an idea into a prephysical reality that becomes ready to manifest in the physical world. Feeling is the *magic ingredient* and the most powerful form available to you is *soul-based joy*. Rather than just stirring up feelings about the desired outcome, tune into the joy which naturally flows from your soul and add that to the intention you have defined. Ideally, an equal balance between the amount of intent and feeling makes for the most powerful act of creativity. When both aspects of consciousness are used in equal balance, intertwining intent and feeling together in one creative act, then *magic happens!*

3. Motion is the final component in the formula and that means taking action. But first, paradoxically, you need to *wait and let it incubate*. Let it all go out of your conscious awareness for several days. This allows your soul level of consciousness to go to work on it and give it the power that an act of true creation requires. Then, as the energy of your environment begins to reorganize itself around the emerging new reality, you can provide the third and final component – physical action. Synchronistic flow will begin to appear in your life: "Coincidences" will occur which cause events around you to move towards the fulfillment of your desired goal. When this flow of supportive coincidences begins to occur, your task is to provide the action which each synchronistic event requires, until the goal has become fully manifested. Most often, goals materialize through a daisy chain of events and opportunities, each of which builds up to the final realization of the entire, original goal.

Example: Man Seeks Woman

A good example of the use of powerful creativity is in the attraction of a mate. Let's say, for instance, that Tom is a 40-year-old widower who has been through a difficult time recovering from his loss. Now, finally, he's ready to go looking for love, hopefully in all the right places.

Let's see how Tom can apply the principles of true creativity, and at the same time, we'll watch out for the pitfalls that he could encounter.

Step 1: Thought

Tom makes up a mental list of all the attributes he'd like to find in his new love. He'd like similar interests and age, and someone who lives within easy reach of his location. (On a personal note, when I was searching, I deliberately didn't specify location. I did find my true love, but I also found myself commuting a thousand miles a week for several months before we moved in together. So consider whether you'll have the time to invest if a distance becomes involved. Also, know that sometimes it helps to expand the area to have more options.) More than anything, Tom would like to meet someone who simply appreciates him for who he is. If Tom gets too specific, he could eliminate the best possible person from the list of potentials. What if he defines height and his ideal mate is an inch taller than him? Sorry, Tom, you'd miss by an inch! I recommend defining just the most important attributes. You want to leave the universe the wiggle space to be able to find your best match.

Step 2: Feeling

To create, you need to aim for the *expansive* variety of feeling. Its opposite, *contractive* feeling, is called that because its focus is self-centered. Contractive feeling feeds inwards toward "Me, me, me, and what I want," while expansive feeling includes benefits to others. Another pitfall to guard against is having a feeling of desperate need. Neediness will drive away a positive result as it is a constant affirmation of the *lack* of something. If Tom felt needy, he would inadvertently create more lack in his life. So what's he to do? The simplest way is for him to focus on the expansive form of feeling by including ways that others will benefit as well as himself. Tom needs to imagine, not only himself being filled with joy at meeting his ideal mate, but also imagine her being overjoyed at meeting someone exactly like him. Once two or more people are in the picture, you have expansive feeling and that condition will feed vital life energy into the ideas that were defined in Step 1.

Step 3: Action

Tom will allow his soul and the universe time to digest his new creation and begin to manifest its possibilities. He will then begin to look for ideas about places to go to meet new people. His inner wisdom will feed him ideas, and the more Tom pays attention to these, the more he will notice synchronicity happening in his life. It can be an eye-opening experience when you follow intuition-based ideas, as you often don't see the point of taking a certain initial path of action until later when the point becomes apparent.

Other examples of powerful creativity changing your life for the better include the creation of abundance in all aspects of your life – in financial ways, in vibrant health, and in lasting friendships with others. In every case, the creation of a new picture of reality will instigate a chain of synchronistic events leading to the fulfillment of the vibrant dream that you have brought into being.

The Spiritual Age

The Spiritual Age

The Spiritual Age is not just another age to be documented in the pages of history books.

> *The Spiritual Age is a quantum leap
> in the evolution of humankind.*

There are 12 distinct stages in the evolution of human consciousness, and these are listed later in this book. There is a lower tier of six material stages followed by a higher tier of six spiritual stages. Once a person shifts from the material tier into the spiritual tier of evolution, everything changes. The old rules no longer apply, and the ways of the new reality have to be understood and acted upon.

Imagine the radical change that a butterfly goes through in its transformation from an earthbound, limited chrysalis to the joyous freedom of a butterfly. Likewise, a radical transformation occurs when humans move into the spiritual stages of their evolution.

When you enter the realms of spiritual consciousness through the gateway of the heart, you begin to understand that love is more important than money, power, fame, or any of the other entrapments of material life.

Love, Light, Laughter

Upon moving into the energy of unconditional love, it becomes clear that helping others is the key to success in life. Your viewpoint of life is expanded, just as the butterfly sees more from its position above the ground than it ever saw before while earthbound.

In the New Reality, success will be measured, not by money, but by the amount of joy in your life.

Once a person has gained an understanding of the expanded realm of the heart, they are free to move on to the next stages of spiritual consciousness. Inspiration starts to flow. Inner knowing comes to the fore. Intuition is your daily guide and helper as the wisdom of your soul comes forth to help you succeed at all your efforts in life.

With soul communion comes the blissful joy of spiritual consciousness. With that blissful joy comes inner peace and the lifting away of all the cares of the world. This is reality. This is the state that God always intended for you to discover so that you can live and love in the light of soul consciousness and become a fully-empowered spiritual being.

Your birthright is love, light, and the laughter that springs from spiritual joy.

The
Expanded
View of God

The Expanded View of God

Life used to be so much simpler. Today, the more we learn about the huge expanse of the universe, the more we realize what we *don't* know.

Back in the Middle Ages, people saw Earth as flat. They saw the stars as having been set in the sky above us simply as decoration, and God was viewed as very much an individual, a father-figure who watched over us from somewhere up in that sky.

As a child, I was taught to view God in the same way. We were taught that same image of a human-like God who personally watched over each and every one of us. That was before the Hubble Space Telescope started to show us how incredibly huge the universe is. In the decades since, our appreciation of the size of the universe has increased enormously. As a result, our view of the size of the Creator of the universe has increased enormously.

Today, most people have shifted from a human-like image of God to one of an ever-present spirit which is behind all things. There is, by definition, no part of the universe where an ever-present being cannot exist. Therefore, we can reason that God, as an omnipresent being, must be at least the size of the entire universe.

Love, Light, Laughter

By current estimates, the universe contains over a hundred billion galaxies, each one containing an estimated two hundred billion suns. That means that there are countless trillions of planets, each one filled with the all-pervasive presence of that which created them. This brings us to today's prevalent spiritual dilemma.

With God's presence being so far-reaching, how can there be any semblance of the personal attention that we were taught to expect from a father-like God image? Today, you are left wondering whether God is: (a) personal, or (b) so large in scale as to be infinitely impersonal. Surely, one idea would exclude the other.

Or would it? Can God be infinite in size and personal as well? The answer lies within the Paradox of Infinite Being.

The Paradox of Infinite Being

The Paradox of Infinite Being

A paradox is something that contains opposite state-ments and yet both are true. The secret to solving para-doxes is to start using the word "and" instead of "or." The question is not whether God is infinitely large or personal. The question becomes, how can God be infi-nite in size and personal as well?

Look at it this way; we know that God is an ever-present consciousness. In Bible study, the three O's define God as *Omnipresent, Omnipotent, and Omniscient.*

Love, Light, Laughter

The attributes of being all-present, all-powerful, and all-knowing tell you that God always was an infinite field of consciousness. He was only ever portrayed as a human-type figure because people in olden times felt more at home with the idea.

God is ever-present, therefore nothing can exist outside of God because God has to be in everything. To be beyond everything finite, it follows that God must be infinite.

An infinite field of consciousness could be aptly referred to as an Infinite Being, as long as the word "Being" is used in the sense of an ultimate state of consciousness, and not in the sense of a human-like being.

If nothing exists beyond the consciousness of Infinite Being, then the universe was formed within its consciousness. Therefore, God or Infinite Being is greater than the universe.

I remember being told in science class at school that space must be infinite in size because there couldn't be anything beyond the end of space; therefore, it had to go on forever. It didn't sound right at the time, and now I know why. Space is actually finite, because it was created within Infinite Being. The created must be less than its creator; therefore, space must be less than infinite.

The universe is finite.
Beyond the envelope of space exists only
the consciousness which created it.

In order to create the universe, Infinite Being came forth into action and divided the "waters" of its consciousness into two complementary aspects: *Creator* and *Preserver*. In the West, we are used to thinking of the Creator as God the Father, while the Preserver aspect is called the Holy Spirit. In the East, the names are different but the principles are exactly the same. For example, the Hindu name for the Creator aspect of God is *Brahma,* while *Vishnu* represents the aspect of God that preserves and sustains the universe.

Before we reach the solution to the Paradox of Infinite Being, let's take a moment to see how legends of Creation from all over the world share that common thread of two complementary aspects coming together to bring light into existence.

Legends
of Creation

Legends of Creation

Most religions and spiritual cultures hold an image of God the Creator which falls into one of these three forms:

1. A single creative entity. This is a unified view of God which, for simplicity, ignores the different facets of consciousness that were needed to create the universe and, instead, focuses on the One.

2. A duality, where God employs two aspects of itself in order to achieve the Creation of the universe. Creation myths from around the world mention a dividing of the "waters" of original consciousness.

3. A trinity, where the two aspects of consciousness are activated by a third principle, motion, as in the motion initiated by the original creative command, "Let there be light."

In ancient Greece, the universe was said to have been a place without light until Eros (Love) arose, bringing light and order. Here we have intent and feeling bringing light into being.

In the ancient Aztec culture, an original 'Lord' and 'Lady' of Creation were said to have brought into existence all things. People throughout history have more easily understood humanized, parental versions of God. After all, concepts like God the Father and the Divine Mother have, in the past, been more understandable than face-less, fundamental principles.

In the early days of the Christian religion, competing bishops voted for a unified creed. This resulted in the Holy Trinity of Christianity being composed of God the Father (as the "thought" or creative principle), the Holy Spirit (as the feeling principle), and God the Son (as a representative of God's action upon earth).

Hinduism, the origin of which pre-dates recorded history, recognizes an original or Absolute state as the one ultimate state of being behind all things. Then, from the single-state Absolute, sprang forth the three principles of Creation. These principles are portrayed as the personalities of *Brahma, Vishnu* and *Shiva.*

While Brahma is the Creator aspect which provided the thought or intention that made the universe, Vishnu represents the aspect that preserves and sustains the universe – an all-pervasive love, in other words. Shiva represents the aspect that brings motion into the universe, making possible the creation and the eventual decay of objects in the physical world. Shiva, therefore, can be best understood as the principle of motion which brings constant change.

Judaism, Christianity and Islam all share the same historic roots. In the Book of Genesis, it is said that Creation began when God created the heavens and the earth and then said, "Let there be light." Notice that this initial act of Creation came before the creation of the stars and the creation of our Sun. Therefore, these initial instances of the words "heavens" and "earth" need to be taken metaphorically, not literally. The "earth" was said to be formless and empty, like a pre-creational void, as the Spirit of God hovered over the "waters" of the formless deep. So, here we have:

1. **The intent of God the Creator**, hovering over:

2. **The formless deep of a universe-to-be**. This "formless deep" referred to the universe, not to the Earth, because the stars (and therefore the Earth) had not yet been formed. There was only the principle of feeling, holding the concept of space within a controlled envelope. Then, all possibilities began with:

3. **"Let there be light."** This is where motion was applied in order to activate the hollow shell of the universe. This, then, made all of Creation possible, including the stars, the planets, their biospheres and all that they contain.

The common thread in all of the above stories of Creation is this: Intent and love together created a universe in the form of a void, an abyss. Intent and love were then set into complementary motion in order to bring light and life into the void.

God Is Just a Thought Away

God Is Just a Thought Away

Through the interaction of these two aspects of original consciousness – *Intent* and *Love,* or *Thought* and *Feeling* – the universe was formed and, along with it, the capability for Infinite Being to observe itself from an infinite number of viewpoints in time and space.

The human race today represents approximately seven billion different viewpoints of the one Source. According to the rules of the human adventure, we were born with *spiritual amnesia.* In other words, we have forgotten our inner connection. The challenge of the game of human life is to discover and consciously reconnect to that which, in reality, we always were connected.

Self-awareness and free will are included in the rules of the game. The illusion of separateness from each other is created by an intense focus upon life in an outer, physical world, as viewed by the five senses. In this outer world, people are free to choose to interact with other people in the ways that they see best.

People can choose to believe that they are separate from the ultimate Source to which they are connected. For instance, atheists claim to lack belief, but atheism actually is a belief. If people have an inbuilt connection to

God, yet believe that they don't, then they are actually expressing a belief in something that isn't so, and not a lack of belief.

Mystics talk of experiencing a sense of oneness with the infinite while in deep meditation. Those who can go still deeper into the realms of consciousness report that there is more to it than just a feeling of oneness. Deep within, you aren't so much an individual who is as one with Infinite Being. Deep within, you *are* Infinite Being!

You are Infinite Being observing itself through the one viewpoint that is you. You aren't a *part* of Infinite Being. You *are* Infinite Being, acting from one specific point of view. Likewise, all sentient beings are also Infinite Being, observing themselves from their own unique points of view.

It seems strange to live in a world where everything appears separate and then discover that, beneath all of the surface appearances, we really are One. If you suspend the sense of strangeness that this concept brings long enough to reach some conclusions, you can see that:

1. Friends, acquaintances and strangers alike are all aspects of the One, just as you are. Whatever you do to others upon the stage of this theater of life, you really are doing to yourself!

2. You can never fail to become one with God because you always were God. How could you fail to become yourself? How could God ever reject you or judge you when you are the eyes and ears of God itself, walking through life in this world of manifestation, learning from what you were sent here to experience? The only way that God could reject you is if God decided to stop loving itself, and that's just not going to happen!

The solution to the Paradox of Infinite Being is that while we are a part of an immense universe of almost unlimited proportions, we are also Infinite Being itself. As you experience life through your eyes and ears and senses, you are Infinite Being, acting through one viewpoint of the infinite variety of life. Every fiber of your body is Infinite Being, every dream that you manifest is Infinite Being in action, every tear of joy that you shed is a tear shed by Infinite Being in its form as you.

You can be closer to God than ever before when you realize that every part of your body, mind and spirit is God.

Even in this strange world where we appear
to be separate from everyone else,
the conscious awareness of the presence
of God is a mere thought away.

Positive Transformation

Positive Transformation

As I've explained, we are here on Earth today, separated from the memory of our Divine connection, with a mission to find our way back to that from which we came. People are awakening to that mission. This is the climax of the adventure of human life on Earth. We are becoming aware of our spiritual nature and beginning to explore the expanded realms of awareness which open up to us as we embrace the New Spirituality. Ahead of us lies the manifestation of all of the incredible potential that we have as self-empowered individual aspects of God.

As we live our lives today, we face the great wonder that we are a part of a transformation that will be viewed retrospectively as The Great Change, or simply The Shift. To be a part of this transformation is to be a part of God's plan for humankind upon Earth. This is the time when all of our past experiences are coming together to make possible one great climactic step forward in human evolution.

When the Earth has finished moving into the new, higher energy level, everything will be different. Compared to the old days, it will be as though a great weight has been lifted from above our heads. We will be able to attune

Love, Light, Laughter

ourselves with the divine spirit within and attune ourselves with each other with such ease that we will wonder why we hadn't been living life this way all along.

A Vision
of the
New Earth

A Vision of the New Earth

A great shift to a higher consciousness has been accelerating since the 1960s. The progressive portion of humanity is stretching the envelope of human consciousness deep into new territory. As The Shift progresses over the decades ahead, intuition will bloom and people will begin to notice that their five senses have acquired a new subtlety. The Earth will be seen as more beautiful than ever, filled with subtleties of color and perfumes that were always there and yet were never before detected. The spirit of humanity will be focused on peace and hope for a new tomorrow, which will unfold as if it were the arrival of heaven on earth.

Tomorrow's humanity will develop in the direction of cooperation, not competition. People will treat other people as loved ones and as if they were dear family, because they will see the light within each other and know that we are all connected. That which used to be a burden will now become a joy, as people work to help each other and support each other.

Gone will be the old way of focusing primarily upon materialistic gain, because people, being heart-centered, will want everyone to have everything that they need and everything that helps make life a joyful experience.

Love, Light, Laughter

On the technology front, energy will one day be clean and plentiful after we learn to tap into and convert the life-giving etheric energy that flows from the Sun. Etheric energy has been utilized for thousands of years in non-technological applications under the names chi, prana, and universal life force. It is the primary energy of the Sun, while physical sunlight is its relatively minor secondary energy. Nikola Tesla, the inventor of today's alternating current power systems, experimented with etheric energy, recognized that it behaved quite differently to electric power, and described it as 'cold electricity.'

It is less than 200 years since the key principles of electric energy were discovered. When the principles of its big brother, etheric energy, are mastered, the door can potentially be opened to a wide variety of long sought-after technologies. These can include abundant clean energy, gravitational shielding, magnetic space vehicle propulsion, protective force screens, teleportation, and, because etheric energy is vital life energy, a wide array of advanced healing technology.

Eventually, all forms of toxicity will be addressed and remedied. Gone will be thoughtless pollution by toxic chemicals and the smoke of burning fuels. Gone will be the toxicity of human suffering that pollutes the mental atmosphere which we all share. Gone will be the toxicity of fear and all of its disempowering manifestations.

Love will be the way, and The Way will be Love. People will see the God within others and hold a sense of allowance for everyone to pursue their own unique spiritual path. Gone will be the rivalries of small-minded religious factions. The new vision of the nature of God will be universal and all-inclusive.

Gone will be the personal need to exert a firm control over life, as the fears which cause this will dissolve and softly drift away with the wind.

Humanity will build a world of great beauty in harmony with nature. Nature itself will be honored as a beautiful expression of the Creator. People will give thanks to the consciousness of the Mother Earth which supports us and to the consciousness of the Sun which continually nourishes us with life-giving energy. Most of all, people will give thanks to consciousness of God for life itself and for the joy that communion with the Divine Spirit brings to our very souls and to our deepest sense of being.

The Mirror of Life

The Mirror of Life

There are two ways that humankind can address the mission of finding its way back to the divine source from which we came. We can stretch this mission out to be long and laborious, or with a little forethought, we can make it relatively easy. The choice, as individuals, is ours.

All life operates within the Principle of Reflectance, which guarantees that a universe which is set into motion will always remain in perfect balance. The Principle of Reflectance is often called, and often misunderstood as, the "Law of Karma."

The Principle of Reflectance simply states that every action causes an equal and opposite reaction. It's that simple. It's not a judgment about anything. It just states that every thought, every feeling, and every deed causes the potential for its equal to be reflected back into your life. This is how you continually create your own reality.

The idea that karma can be judgmental in nature seems to spring from the idea that God will judge you after you leave this world. Thanks to today's many volumes of independent research into what actually happens in afterlife experiences, we now know that there is no judgment by God or any being outside of yourself. Pioneering researchers such as Michael Newton and Dolores Cannon have compiled thousands of cases to show that what does happen in the afterlife is a review which is conducted by you as your soul consciousness.

This review is not judgmental at all. It's just a review, the same as any review that comes after the completion of a project. The tone of the review is loving, support-ive, and insightful. Through this process, you are able to see how you learned more about the dispensation of love and service to others in this life. Through this pro-cess, you begin to see ways that you could learn even more about love and service when your time comes to next reincarnate.

> *Helping others through love and service*
> *is the key to sure spiritual advancement*
> *in today's emerging New Reality.*

The Principle of Reflectance states, quite simply, that what you put out comes back. Or to quote the old adage, "What goes around comes around."

This potential energy pattern – your "karma" – is car-ried like a magnetic influence within your energy field until circumstances make its manifestation possible. As we will see, you can determine how life will treat you simply by pre-loading your karmic pattern with the kind of potential which you wish to see manifest.

Three Steps
to a
Better Life

Three Steps to a Better Life

Intention and *attention* are creative actions which affect your karmic pattern. You're always paying attention to something, and those thoughts and actions are, by their very nature, creative. By first setting an intention – focusing on a desired objective and paying attention to how it can become manifest – you add to your own personal reality in ways that you see as desirable. Your intention focuses your attention into a narrower, more defined course of action and therefore makes that action more powerful and effective.

It's the same as a focused beam of light. Some handheld flashlights are designed so that you can adjust their light beams to be either spread wide or focused down into a very tight circle. The focused circle is much brighter, and relatively more powerful in its effects, than the scattered wide beam. A small amount of energy can be focused even more when it's projected as a tiny laser beam. A laser beam is so focused and aligned that it has the power to reach all the way to the moon and reflect back again.

Focus and alignment in one direction add effective power. Intention provides focus to your thoughts and actions, making them more effective.

Love, Light, Laughter

You can use intention to set your focus upon any desired objective to improve your life. You can, for example, steer your life in a direction of spiritual discovery and the expansion of your true potential simply by making the time for spiritual study and practice.

By spending quality time in spiritual activity, you are taking a large step towards your inner God-consciousness. When you take one step towards your inner God-presence, it will take two steps towards you, making your life more inspired and filled with knowing.

Be aware that your thoughts and feelings are creative. You can add anything you want to your life simply through intention and attention. The converse effect is also true. You can inadvertently add something that you don't want in your life simply through worrying about it. Worry will funnel energy into helping create the very situation that you are trying to avoid. When you find yourself worrying unduly about something, raise your mood by thinking thoughts of gratitude for all the good things in your life and you will neutralize and dissipate the lower-frequency thoughts of worry.

Intention is like a magic wand that you can wave to initiate transformation in your life. Whatever you want to add to your life – peace, prosperity, vitality, spiritual joy, or all of these – the change begins with intention.

As we have seen before with the fundamental Law of Creation, there are three main steps to creating a better life. These can be summarized as:

1. **Thought**, or intention, which defines your goal for change.

2. **Feeling**. You add the magic ingredient of soul-based joy.

3. **Motion**. You add action to the equation and act out your inner guidance as to how to manifest such change.

However, none of this will work if there are blockages in the way. Life is complex and the path to the perfect life is often strewn with blockages which slow down your progress. In order to achieve the perfect life, these blocks need to be dissolved and transformed out of the way.

In the computer world, we used to say, "GIGO," meaning "Garbage In, Garbage Out," to point out that the automation of a dysfunctional manual process would only speed up the mess.

In the spiritual world, you need only remember the word "KICK," to remind you to *Kick out the blocks that stand in the way of your progress.*

Kicking Out
the Blocks

Kicking Out the Blocks

Blockages can get in the way of anything that's fun and worth doing. They need to be identified and transformed so that you can get on with your life and find the happiness that everyone truly deserves in this adventure called human life.

To identify blockages, we can use extremely positive statements as triggers that will reveal underlying beliefs.

First, put yourself into a quiet reflective state and, to really push this idea to the limit, state to yourself,

"I am brilliant, gorgeous, and fabulous!"

What happens then? Chances are, due to the social environment that most of us grew up in, you were taught to never make such claims because there's supposed to be something-or-other wrong with thinking that way.

Well, sure, if a child runs the risk of becoming a raving, unsociable egomaniac, then there would be something wrong with thinking that way. But as an adult with a developing sense of spiritual consciousness, ego issues are no longer the point.

Love, Light, Laughter

The point today is to develop your potential and become everything that you can be.

In a healthy, heart-centered society, everyone will be either brilliant, gorgeous and fabulous already or well on their way to becoming so. And the rest of society will be cheering them on in every attempt that they make to improve their lives. After all, wouldn't you rather live among people who are brilliant, gorgeous, fabulous, and supportive than among people who aren't?

Remember, in a heart-centered society, the theme of popular thought would be one of support, not competition. They wouldn't want *anyone* to fail. They'd want everyone to succeed at everything because then there's more of everything for everyone in that society.

Competition constrains. Cooperation expands.

Now, let's come back to present-day reality, where we are building a cooperative future step-by-step. As you probably just saw, your blockages emerge when you say wonderful things about yourself.

When you say, *"I am brilliant, gorgeous, and fabulous!"* what thoughts come up to the surface of your mind?

Probably a lot of *"Yes, but I don't feel..."* statements.

Those are your blockages, or limiting beliefs. Here's how to dissolve them so that they won't limit your happiness any longer.

*Having identified a blockage and brought it
out into the open where it can be worked on,
you use energy work to transform it
out of your life once and for all.*

Dissolving Limiting Beliefs

Dissolving Limiting Beliefs

Your heart has a wonderful ability to transform limiting beliefs by the application of its natural frequency of consciousness, which is that of *unconditional love.*

While your physical heart is tucked away behind your rib cage, the *energy center* of your heart is outside of your body, just in front of your breastbone. It is here that the frequency of heart-centered consciousness is focused. Visualize this energy center as a small sphere of brilliant white light four inches (ten centimeters) in front of the center of your chest.

Imagine the air being filled with vital life energy, like a white mist that fills the space around you. The air actually is filled with vital life energy, but the point of the exercise is to draw additional quantities of this energy in to add extra power to your heart's energy center.

How will you be able to direct the flow of this vital life energy? As a primary energy, it is closer to the frequencies of mind than any secondary, physical energy. You will be able to attract it, concentrate it, and direct it simply through the application of mental pressure. Your imagination is your creative faculty, so use visualization to create and apply the mental pressure that will direct the life energy.

Like physical light, vital life energy comes in a variety of colors depending upon its frequency. By visualizing it as a white light, which is formed by the combination of all colors, you guarantee that you will be working with a balanced energy that consists of all frequencies.

Prepare to draw quantities of it into your heart's energy center using your mental power of visualization. As you take a deep breath, see the mist-like vital life energy that fills the air being drawn into your lungs. Now that you have extra life energy within you, direct it outwards into your heart's energy center just in front of your chest. On the outbreath, see the white light of this focused, vital life energy charging the energy center with its brilliant power. Do this for a total of five in-breaths and out-breaths.

Now that your heart's energy center is charged with intense life energy, use its natural frequency of unconditional love to transform each blockage in turn. Whatever blockage you identified, say to yourself mentally:

> *"I release the belief that [blockage statement]*
> *and transform it into the light now.*
> *I replace that old belief with*
> *the knowing that I am loved*
> *and that I am Love."*

For example, "I release the belief that <u>money is bad</u> and transform it into the light now. I replace that old belief with the knowing that I am loved and that I am Love."

Notice that you don't have to state the opposite of the old belief. You just transform it and release it using the energy of unconditional love as the transformative power.

However, releasing the old belief creates an absence, or a vacuum, that wants to be filled. Replace the old belief with the pure unconditional Love which flows throughout the universe and fill this vacuum with positive energy.

The statement, *"knowing that I am loved,"* is an affirmation of your awareness that the universe is filled with the love of God and that you only have to tune into this love to feel its power and eternal support.

Everything and everyone exists in a universe
filled with unconditional love.
It's the way the universe was designed.

From Fear
to
Natural Flow

From Fear to Natural Flow

Control issues are based upon fear. Often the cause of that fear is forgotten but the need to stay in control of one's environment still remains.

When you find yourself in a group of people, sometimes someone will make a suggestion as to what the group could do next. If you find it difficult to go along with another person's suggestion, then you may be experiencing a fear of being out of control. In that case, some type of conditioning, at some time, taught you that it's safer to be in full control of, not only yourself, but everything around you.

The great thing about the energetic release technique in the previous chapter is that you don't have to spend months or years trying to discover the exact cause of something like this; you just have to identify it and release it. Say to yourself mentally:

> *"I release the belief that <u>I need to be in control</u>*
> *and transform it into the light now.*
> *I replace that old belief with the knowing*
> *that I am loved and that I am Love."*

Love, Light, Laughter

Just repeating that release technique on several occasions can bring enormous release from the underlying fear that causes the need to be in control of everything around you. It also helps when you understand what it means to be *allowing* rather than *controlling*.

When life is lived in the flow of natural, perfect timing, you are experiencing a phenomenon called *flow*. This is a stream of consciousness which comes from your full, inner consciousness out through your conscious mind and into expression in the physical world. Flow results in your being able to reach achievements far beyond your usual potential.

Let your conscious mind allow your full, inner consciousness to prompt you as to what actions are appropriate and when. There is a time and a place for everything, and there is a *best* time and place for anything you wish to achieve. Your inner soul consciousness has the tools to see when and where your efforts can ideally produce the best results. Let go of that nagging fear that you have to be in conscious control. Trust the full aspect of your consciousness to let you know what works best and when.

Your inner soul consciousness is the full aspect of you. It is the world's best expert on what is best for you to achieve next because it is you. No advisor knows better about you than your inner you. No other advisor is there for you 24 hours a day, 7 days a week. The trick is to open up to your greater range of consciousness. That is achieved by going within, by noting the impressions that your intuition will provide, and by being willing to live in the flow of perfect, natural timing.

Then, suddenly, instead of feeling like you are swimming against the tide, you find that life flows in a wonderful and meaningful manner. Everything will come together to support your efforts at the exact time that everything is needed. You'll have achieved *natural flow*.

The Evolution
of Human
Consciousness

The Evolution of Human Consciousness

The human race was designed to evolve through 12 progressive stages of consciousness, all the way from caveman to cosmic consciousness. The 12-Stage Map of Human Consciousness consists of two tiers of six stages each. It begins with a Material Tier of six stages and then progresses into a Spiritual Tier of another six stages. In brief, the 12 stages are:

The Material Tier

1. Survival: Maintaining physical existence

2. Tribal: Gathering into groups for protection

3. Courage: Adventure and exploration

4. Conformity: Order out of chaos through hierarchical control

5. Intellect: Basic mental development, physical science

6. Community: Ecological consciousness, putting the greater good above self

The Spiritual Tier

7. Love: Heart-centered consciousness, the first step in spiritual consciousness

8. Inspiration: Higher mental development, attunement with the age-old wisdom of your soul

9. Creativity: The ability to successfully create a better reality

10. Enlightenment: The immediate goal of spiritual seekers, direct access to the secrets of the universe

11. Angelic: The realm of angels and avatars

12. Cosmic: The peak of human experience and the first step in growing to become part of the consciousness of a planet

Today, most of the human race is approaching Stage 7, the gateway to spiritual consciousness. Meanwhile, the leading portion of humanity is already in Stage 7 and exploring Stages 8 and 9.

The title of this book, *Love, Light, Laughter*, refers to Stages 7, 8 and 9. These stages encompass unconditional love, the light of knowledge obtained through inspiration, and the joy of contact with the powerful creativity of your soul.

In the future lie the final stages of spiritual development. The human journey from caveman to cosmic consciousness is one that begins with relatively unconscious, disconnected individuals searching until they discover the road back to the place from which they came. The formerly unconscious human then learns enough about life to eventually return to the embrace of God as a conscious god, fully empowered with the love and wisdom which springs from the divine source of all life.

Goodbye
to Guilt

Goodbye to Guilt

Problems are created by the sense of separation which pervades the material stages of consciousness. These problems can be healed by the sense of integration experienced in the spiritual stages of consciousness.

A sense of guilt is very common in the material stages of consciousness. In these, guilt can run rampant, causing severe limitation in a person's path of spiritual development. A sense of guilt can spring from a real cause, such as a failure to live up to an obligation to help another person, or it can have its roots in imaginary fears. After all, guilt is one of the many manifestations of fear.

For example, a person can worry that they may be spiritually inadequate, even a sinner, perhaps. This creates the fear that God will not love them.

Such thoughts are created within the material range of consciousness. However, upon moving into the spiritual stages of consciousness, the reality changes radically. It's as if, in the spiritual world, the opposite is true. Instead of worrying about a lack of God's love, your main challenge is to channel the unlimited love which fills the universe without being too distracted from your daily life by all of this wonderful energy.

Love, Light, Laughter

One of the main sources of guilt in modern society is the idea that humankind once fell from grace, and therefore it is fundamentally flawed. The question is, are we descended from sinners or are we simply part of an adventure where we explore life in a particularly realistic way thanks to our spiritual disconnection? I think that the answer lies, oddly enough, with the Ford Motor Company!

The Ford Motor Company has built millions of cars over the decades. Some of them have later been found to have defects. Invariably, serious defects have led to complete recalls of the affected cars so that the faults can be promptly corrected.

Now, if a manufacturer of cars can be so efficient in fixing any defects in the cars they make, why would God be any less efficient in fixing an alleged fault in the creation called humanity? Unless, of course, it's not a *fault* but actually a *design feature*.

God, the Creator of humanity, did not recall humanity to correct the alleged fault of spiritual disconnection. Therefore, it must be a design feature and not a fault. Life as a human is about finding out how to reconnect spiritually under the most realistic and challenging circumstances. And we continually rise to this challenge.

The higher stages of human consciousness are all about the development of spirituality. We are entering those stages of spiritual consciousness today, so wave good-bye to imaginary guilt and move ahead with confidence into the realms of spiritual expansion which lie before you.

The Power of Gratitude

The Power of Gratitude

As I noted in the last chapter, guilt is just another one of the many forms of fear. Anxiety, depression, and anger are some of its other forms of expression.

In today's world, fear is still being promoted by many people for purposes best known to them. The news media, for example, seems to generally believe that the fear factor makes a news story more exciting. Fortunately, fear has a simple antidote. It's called *love*. Love dissolves fear. When fears try to creep into your mind, you can simply invoke love as a counter-measure.

Gratitude is one type of expression of love which has enormous power. Gratitude is invoked when you mentally send love to those whom you appreciate. It becomes especially powerful when you send your gratitude to God for all the good things in your life and for life itself, because God will reciprocate with uplifting energies. That one step you take towards God really does bring a reaction of two steps towards you.

Gratitude takes you right out of your personal sphere of consciousness and into an expanded view of the universe.

Love, Light, Laughter

In this way, it raises you far above the petty fears that still try to haunt the everyday world. Gratitude is one of the most beautiful secrets in spiritual life. It is an expression of love, and love flows through all forms of manifestation. Without love, life in the universe cannot exist. Love is the universal force of preservation which holds Creation in manifestation.

When you allow your heart to open to the universe's flow of love, gratitude comes with that flow. Gratitude for being alive, for just existing, for just being in the flow of the adventure of life. Gratitude for the Sun that gives us life. Gratitude for the Earth that gives us our home in the cosmos. Gratitude for the people that you love, and for those who share your journey through life.

Gratitude flows unimpeded from an open heart. When you allow it, gratitude will flow as freely as the sunshine, unobstructed by judgments or conditions.

Use the following affirmation and see what happens. Keep repeating it and, each time, think more about what the words mean.

The Gratitude Affirmation adds new meaning to the words, "Quality of life." It really works! Try it now.

Gratitude Affirmation

I am grateful for life
And all that I love
I am grateful for the Earth
And the Sun up above
I am grateful for my spirit
And my inner being
For the One that I express
And the joy of this feeling

Finding Freedom

Finding Freedom

If you were struggling to pay bills, you would want to create a natural level of prosperity in your life and end the struggle. But if you had a subconscious blockage that said, "Money is bad," then the blockage would prevail and you'd continue to struggle.

From a neutral, detached point of view, it is obvious that money, which is just another form of energy, can't actually be "bad" any more than electricity is bad. Functionally, money is no more than the currency of personal energy. It represents the work you've done and your ability to pay for the work of others to supply your needs. If you have a blockage about money, then it's time to stop suffering and kick out the block!

In centuries past, it was very common for spiritual seekers to take vows as nuns or monks in order to dedicate their lives to attaining closer communion with God. Vows of poverty, chastity and obedience were taken, and such vows made perfect sense at the time and in that environment.

Unfortunately, they were usually taken with no expiry date. There was no "until death do us part" type of clause included in the vows, so these individuals' subconscious minds faithfully recorded the vows as obligations which would continue indefinitely.

Born again, and again, and again

However, the human experience was designed to be an evolutionary adventure through not just one life, but through many incarnations. Thanks to the pioneering efforts of researchers such as Brian Weiss and Dolores Cannon, it has now become common knowledge that reincarnation is simply one of the facts of life. It's no longer a matter of belief, as the cumulative evidence is overwhelming.

Brian Weiss was a traditional psychotherapist until one of his clients started to recall past-life traumas which held the key to her nightmares and anxiety attacks. Then, she began to bring forth messages from the afterlife which contained remarkable information. He developed a type of past-life therapy in order to treat this patient and suddenly found himself beginning a new phase in his career. Today, he is a world-renowned expert on past-life therapy and he has also developed a form of present-life therapy using hypnotic progressions into probable *future* lives.

Dolores Cannon is another pioneer who has been waking the Western world up to reincarnation. She has been a hypnotist since the 1960s and began past-life regression work in 1979. She has broken new ground by developing many deep hypnosis-inducing tools. Today, thousands of case studies later, she is a prolific author and a leading authority on past-life regression.

We are here on earth to be a part of the entire human experience as it progresses throughout the centuries and the millennia. We, as the evolving human race, are here to learn and progress from a wide variety of experiences and we do that by reincarnating into different environments in different time eras.

You plan each life

As souls, we make a plan for each incarnation ahead of time. This is done in cooperation with the rest of our immediate soul group and also our extended soul family. One of the joys of recalling past life experiences is to discover the love that you shared in past lives with the very same people who are special to you in this life. Close friends are typically members of your soul family who take on different roles as all of you choose different experiences throughout history.

The memories of these past lives are all faithfully recorded and stored just below your conscious awareness in the vast memory resources of your subconscious mind. If you choose, you can access such memories using a relaxed state of expanded awareness.

Such states of expanded awareness are easy to achieve. They happen all the time – when you are absorbed by a story on television or in a book, or when you are in "auto pilot" mode on a long drive. The same relaxed state of expanded awareness can, with the appropriate intention, recall the subconscious memories of your choice, whether those memories are from this life or from a past life.

Let obsolete baggage go

If you have taken a vow of poverty, chastity and obedience in a past life, then it can still be active in your subconscious mind today. If the vow was taken with no expiry date, then its effects can actively interfere with your happiness in today's world.

The effects of such a vow in today's world will create blockages to your personal growth. The poverty part will produce financial hardship. The chastity part will make relationships unfulfilling.

The obedience part leads to a belief that people who have gained positions of authority know best. This self-denying stance is no longer appropriate in today's world, as these are the days when the Spiritual Age is emerging. Today, we live in a self-empowered age which calls for individual mastery of life and not the blind following of anyone who claims to know best.

Sooner or later, all such obsolete baggage needs to be released in order to set your soul free from the invisible chains of self-imposed limitation.

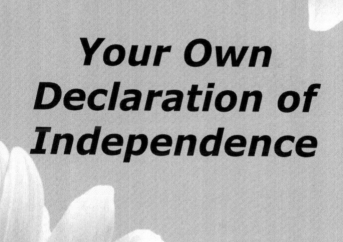

*Your Own
Declaration of
Independence*

Your Own Declaration of Independence

As you've seen, any vows taken in past lives with no expiry date are often inappropriate in the way they affect later lives. The circumstances that made a past life vow appropriate at the time no longer exist because every life is a different adventure in a different setting.

In order to develop your own potential, you need to be free of unnecessary and limiting obligations. Only *you* can develop your potential. No one else can do it for you. This life is your adventure and your time either to grow to realize your true potential or to be hobbled continually by blockages that slow everything down.

If you suspect that your subconscious mind may be harboring inappropriate vows, you can release them quite simply by conscious effort.

Enter a quiet state and make a necessary and long-overdue statement:

"I now renounce and release all vows that I have taken which have outlived their purposes and which now limit my potential for growth. I reclaim my personal freedom and declare such vows renounced and released as of now. I replace old vows with the knowing that I am loved and that I am Love."

Love, Light, Laughter

You can repeat it two or more times, adding feeling and meaning each time. Continue to re-visit the statement until you feel truly liberated and able to move forward to grow and naturally prosper in these, the dawning days of The Spiritual Age.

The Enlightenment Meditation

The Enlightenment Meditation

Here is a meditation technique that works well even in today's busy world. It is quick, easy and effective in producing deeper states of consciousness. When you need inspiration, here's how to reach it quickly and easily.

Set the purpose of this particular meditation session, whether it is problem-solving or the pursuit of inspiration and enlightenment. Then, consciously detach from that purpose and focus on the technique.

The gateway to spiritual consciousness is through the heart, so that is the entry point to all higher states of consciousness. As mentioned earlier, heart-centered consciousness is typically focused in an energy center, or chakra, outside of the physical body, approximately four inches (ten centimeters) in front of the breastbone. It is a small, whirling vortex of energy operating at a specific frequency of consciousness. This chakra can be used to sense the heart-centered consciousness of others, and it can also be used in transmission mode to send unconditional love to others.

Universal life energy comes from the universe, through the Sun, and fills all of the space around you. On a sunny day, when its presence is especially intense, your eyes can often faintly detect globules of this energy floating in the air as you look up towards the clear sky. To invoke spiritual consciousness, add extra life energy to the heart chakra in order to swiftly activate heart-centered consciousness.

Universal life energy responds immediately to the mental pressure exerted by your will. It can be attracted, conditioned and even transmitted outwards to any desired objective. In order to charge your heart chakra with universal life energy, you visualize it coming into your body on each in-breath.

Close your eyes and see this energy as a white mist permeating the space which surrounds you. Then, see this as a white light entering and filling your lungs as it passes through your nostrils on each in-breath. Draw this life-giving energy into yourself using the power of your will.

Then, on each out-breath, see this concentration of energy as a brilliant white light moving forward into your heart chakra, filling this center of consciousness with intense light and vitality.

Do this for five in-breaths and out-breaths and your consciousness will shift into a heart-centered focus.

Now, focus your awareness into that sphere of white light which fills the heart chakra and feel the love that exists there.

Next, transfer that concentrated sphere of light straight up to the "third eye" energy center, which is positioned between the eyebrows, but two inches (five centimeters) in front of the body. This is a unique energy center in that it combines the light of the Divine Father aspect of the Creator with the love of the Divine Mother aspect. The light of the third eye comes from the all-knowing space within, and this chakra also connects you to the love and support of your Divine source.

Focus your awareness in that enlightened energy center in front of the forehead. Have your head level and your eyes tilted slightly upwards (around 20 degrees) behind closed eyelids.

Everyone has their own concept of God, Infinite Being, or the One Spirit. Use the power of gratitude to generate a response from this, the source of all life. Give thanks to your concept of God for life and then ask for God's love and inspiration to fill your awareness.

The reaction will be immediate, and if you allow it, you will be filled with the wonder of God's love and gentle power.

Give yourself some time in that sacred space and be receptive to helpful ideas that flow into your conscious awareness from your inner being.

Reaching Enlightenment Rapidly

Reaching Enlightenment Rapidly

The Enlightenment Meditation opens up your ability to quickly reach the higher frequency states of consciousness. It works by charging key chakras with additional universal life energy. This energy powers the chakras or energy centers in your subtle energy body, so the more intense you make your visualization of this practice, the more effective it is.

When you attract life energy from your surroundings and breathe it as brilliant white light into your lungs, see it as intensely brilliant and pure. Apply determined mental pressure to draw it in, and, on each out-breath, send it forward to focus it into your heart chakra.

When you express your gratitude by giving thanks to God for life, make it more intense and sincere each time. Gather your emotional energy, project that into the practice, and you will experience greater results each time.

The first stage of enlightenment is the opening of the doorway to intuitive knowledge. The Enlightenment Meditation is an engine of enlightenment. Feed it the best fuel possible and watch the results happen.

Love, Light, Laughter

When you have taken the sphere of awareness up to the third eye and expressed gratitude for life and all of Creation, the next step forward is to open communion with Infinite Being.

Infinite Being is that ultimate state of consciousness which lies even beyond the Creator consciousness. It is the unchanging state of consciousness behind all things.

There are three underlying Principles of Communion that should be noted:

1. Ask and it shall be given. As we live in a free will environment, you have to ask for communion with God before it will be given. The key to experiencing communion, therefore, is simply to ask.

2. Your soul acts as an intermediary in communion. It is connected to both Infinite Being and to your conscious awareness. It opens up the pathway to the communion you request, and it translates the impressions which return into thoughts that your conscious mind can readily understand.

3. The higher you reach in consciousness, the better communion you will experience. Therefore, make it your intention to communicate, via your soul consciousness, all the way to the ultimate state of Infinite Being.

As an analogy, in the computer world, a modem acts as an intermediary between your computer and the Internet. It sends and receives information along a carrier wave that is capable of being transmitted between your computer and the nearest connection point to the Internet.

Similarly, your soul is capable of communication through the higher realms and into the ultimate state of consciousness of Infinite Being itself. As your conscious mind is habitually focused upon the outside world and uses your regular mode of thinking, your soul takes on the task of translating that form of thought to and from realms that are beyond your regular sphere of activity.

In using the modem on your computer, you rarely think about how it helps you to communicate with the Internet. Likewise, with communion, you'll rarely think about how your soul is performing its function to help you communicate with God. You'll just know that your requests for communication are being answered and that the responses are nothing short of inspiring and uplifting.

Enlightenment begins with soul-connected inspiration. The practice of inner communion with God or Infinite Being expands your ability to be inspired continually and to receive intuitive knowledge any time you need it.

Inner Communion With God

Inner Communion With God

Inner communion with God takes you completely out of the mundane world and into a state of spiritual awareness which changes everything. Suddenly, you realize how limited routine daily life can be. Suddenly, you realize that there is a divine plan behind all of existence. And, suddenly, you know what it is that you need to do next in order to expand your consciousness into realms of more spiritual freedom and enlightenment.

No longer will you be limited by lack of divine guidance when you establish communion with God. No longer will you feel that you have a purpose in life but never quite know what it is. No longer will you feel like a boat with no rudder, drifting along the river of life without any special plan.

With inner communion comes purpose. With purpose comes focus and achievement. With achievement comes the knowing that your life on Earth has become a complete and utter success.

You came into this life to experience a spiritual awakening. There is only one task among your list of tasks in each busy day which moves you swiftly towards this goal, and that is spiritual communion.

Love, Light, Laughter

Communion is made possible by entering the quiet space which meditation allows. Retreating from the noise and clatter of daily duties, you can immerse yourself in the peaceful envelope of inner light which meditation brings. By damping down the wild gyrations of the conscious mind and allowing this inner peace to emerge, you prepare yourself to bring true meaning into your spiritual practice.

People have always sought an intermediary between their daily awareness and a state of communion with God. Whether this is achieved through ritual led by ministers or priests, or whether this is sought through an intermediary such as Jesus, people have always known that some sort of connector makes inner communion more available to them.

In today's world, with deeper states of meditation becoming more commonplace, it is now possible to develop communion through your own inner link – *your soul consciousness*. Your soul is connected through the higher spiritual realms, through and beyond the realms of the masters and the angels, to God itself.

By developing communion with your soul, you open up the doorway to communion with every progressive realm of higher consciousness – all the way back to the Creator and Infinite Being itself.

No longer do you have to guess your purpose in life or search for ways to find spiritual fulfillment. No longer do you have to wander through the avenues of material existence, yearning for spiritual liberation.

*Make the contact now with
your divine nature and
you will never again feel
spiritually left alone in this world.*

The experience of communion with God is one which becomes deeper with practice. With every step you take, your communion becomes more profound. With every ascent into the bliss of higher consciousness, you become more subtly enlightened and filled with the love and light which flows freely from God.

Communion with God takes practice. It takes intention. The rewards are there to be experienced. Your spiritual destiny awaits your next steps into the realms of love, light, and laughter that come with soul consciousness.

The
Light
Within

The Light Within

All people have to do to step into today's emerging spiritual consciousness is to discover their hearts.

Once people find the unconditional love within their hearts, they go on to find the light and inspiration that streams continually outwards from their very souls.

Within the light, they discover the laughter – the joy of spiritual contact which fills their very beings with happiness regardless of any external circumstances.

The hallmarks of the New Spirituality are love, light, and laughter. They are the stages of spiritual consciousness which will form the basis of the building of a New Earth. They are the seeds of a greater awareness, a greater love, and a greater understanding for all of the people upon the Earth.

Further
Explorations

Further Explorations

Spiritual understanding fills your mind with light and makes the world a better place to live in.

Infinite Being Insight E-Books by Owen Waters are packed with clear and concise insights into Spiritual Metaphysics.

Insight E-Books are available for immediate download onto your computer or mobile device.

As a service to the spiritual community, a full-size sample e-book is always available *free of charge* at the Infinite Being web site:

www.infinitebeing.com/free

**Add Inspiration
to Your
Weekends**

Add Inspiration to Your Weekends

Owen Waters writes a complimentary spiritual metaphysics newsletter which empowers people to discover new vistas of inspiration, love and creativity.

To receive an inspiring new article on spiritual metaphysics each weekend, sign up for his Free Newsletter at:

www.infinitebeing.com/news

Made in the USA
Lexington, KY
02 February 2010